52 simple, healthful meals based on

vegetable protein, milk and eggs

COOKING
WITH
CONSCIENCE

A Book for People Concerned
About World Hunger

By Alice Benjamin and Harriett Corrigan

With drawings by Ann Gibb

A VINEYARD BOOK
THE SEABURY PRESS · NEW YORK

For JOEL, BILL and DAVID

Third Printing

1982
The Seabury Press
815 Second Avenue
New York, N.Y. 10017

Printed in the United States of America

ISBN: 0-8164-0902-1

Library of Congress Catalog Card Number: 78-51936

CONTENTS

Table of Menus

Table of Menus

Table of Menus

Table of Menus

(Foods in parentheses are suggestions for which no recipe is given.)

Acknowledgments

Innumerable people have been helpful and encouraging to us in the writing of this book. In particular we would like to thank the 52 volunteer cooks and their families and friends who tested our recipes. Most, but not all, were members of Saint Luke's Church, Darien, Connecticut. Their prompt and patient help and many useful suggestions were gratefully received: Dorie Ames, Ann Armiger, Muriel C. Back, The R. C. Baker Family, Grace B. Bender, Arden Broecking, Jill Brown, Joy Chapman, Vidal S. Clay, Mrs. Warren W. Crawford, Su Cross, Mrs. Robert W. Crozier, Anne R. Dunlap, Mr. and Mrs. John W. Franklin, Helen Franklin, Gay Gaston, Betty Geerlings, Mrs. William R. Geery, Marty Gilbert, Lynn F. Glaze, Veronica Grant, Mary Margaret Grubbs, Anne W. Hance, Jimmie and Patsy Harker, Mrs. Kent Haydock and Family, Mrs. James Heinritz, Dorothy Hutton, Sally Sutphin Joslin, Kathy Kenyon, Ruth Lutz, Ruth Mackey, Barbara Marshall, Fay P. Mason, Donna R. Matson, Peg Merrow, Karen Nangle, Maggie Niles, Mrs. Kenneth R. Otis, The Samuel F. Peirce Family, Isabel C. Ray, Louise See, Louise Simons, Nancy D. Sutton, Mrs. Everett P. Walkeley, Shirley Ward, Jane Hamilton West, Herbert B. West, Maria West, Maria Selden West, Mrs. Whitney Williams, Emilie J. Wiggin, and Arvilla Wubbenhorst. We are also grateful for the cooperation and encouragement of the Rev. Robert Nelson Back, Rector of Saint Luke's.

Many long hours were given to the preparation of the manuscript by Elise Maclay, Joan Frank, Dorie Ames and Anne Hance, and valuable culinary advice was given to us on many recipes by Helen Bellamore. As well as appreciating their hard work and high standards, we enjoyed working with them.

Introduction

We are accustomed to eating well. Sometimes too well. Day after day, we sit down to a full meal, eat until we are satisfied, and throw the leftovers away. But we are beginning to be haunted by the fact that in Niger and Mali, Biafra and Bangladesh, Senegal and Chad, and even in sections of our own country, people are hungry. Very hungry. Starving.

Nor is this a matter of a period of famine that will soon be over. Father Hesburgh, President of Notre Dame University and head of the Overseas Development Council, predicts "a food crisis that will make the energy crisis look like a picnic.. a cataclysmic kind of revolution" if we don't act while there is still time. Robert McNamara, President of the World Bank, agrees. Speaking recently on Meet the Press, Mr. McNamara said: "There are going to be millions dying."

Can we love God and man and not care? Rabbi Marc Tannenbaum stated: "For a Nation with our liberal, humanitarian ideals and for a people with our Christian and Jewish heritages to temporize in the face of the greatest challenge in the last decades of the 20th century is to risk the betrayal of everything meaningful we profess to stand for."

But what can one person, one family do? The struggle for food involves whole nations with teeming populations and the problem of sharing the world's food is incredibly complex. Economic systems, storage and distribution, shifting weather patterns, and cultural eating habits all enter in. To think of the magnitude of the problem is paralyzing.

Even so all over America, groups of people are trying to take whatever steps they can to interrupt the process of certain starvation for as many human beings as possible. World food conferences are being held, money is being raised, group efforts are being directed toward effecting compassionate legislation. Not all of us are able to take part in group efforts but there is something that all of us can do: We can eat less grain-fed meat.

Slowly we are beginning to learn that grain-fed meat, especially beef, is a great and unnecessary waste of food resources. For instance, if the United States cut its beef consumption in half, enough grain could be saved to feed 100 million people for a year. The average American uses up five times the agricultural resources of the average African or Indian. We annually feed our livestock as much grain as all the people of China and India eat in a year. Writing in "Harpers Magazine" Frances Moore Lappe says "The world is well beyond the point of being able to support its population with the level of waste on which our diet is based." She calls the American system of protein production and consumption "a system that in the all-inclusiveness of its scope and the banality of its everyday operations appears so normal as to be almost God-given--while in fact it is condemning most of humanity to continual hunger."

Part of the tragedy is that we do not need to eat all that meat for health. A meat-and-potatoes-and-green-vegetable meal is so reassuringly familiar, we choose it almost automatically. But protein, not meat, is the key to health. Whole grains, legumes, and many seeds and vegetables are rich in protein, while milk and eggs use up less of the world's protein resources than meat. If these sources of protein are combined in the right proportions, they can well supply the body's needs. Unfortunately, there is still a great lack of understanding about the need for combining these foods in the right proportions. Beans alone, for instance, do not provide an adequate source of protein. An elementary understanding of how to combine sources of vegetable protein, milk and eggs is one of the main emphases of this book.

There is a growing concern to eat less meat for reasons of conscience. In a recent appeal, Senator Mark Hatfield of Oregon was quite specific: "Some Christians may decide that part of their witness means being a vegetarian. Families can decide how to limit their consumption of beef, perhaps to only certain days or at times of celebration or just on certain days of the week."

Limiting our consumption of meat and giving the money saved to world hunger relief are only partial answers. But they are a beginning. Change begets change. Bread For the World, a Christian citizens' Movement against hunger points out that "Like fasting, meatless meals remind us each week how precious life is and how utterly all of us depend upon the gifts of God."

Whether we change our ways a lot, or only a little, doing so will remind us of the urgency of the problem and will make us, in the words of the familiar grace: "truly mindful of the needs of others."

What this Book Is—and Is Not

Cookbooks abound but they generally fall into broad categories such as basic, gourmet, health, etc. "Cooking with Conscience" falls into none of these categories. In a sense you could call it a fasting cookbook, but since fasting means "not eating for reasons of conscience or religion" that is a contradiction in terms. Yet the book is certainly concerned with eating differently for reasons of conscience. (As the introduction made clear, if we eat less grain-fed meat, we save food and money, which can, at least in small measure, help to alleviate the suffering of the hungry.) But in one sense this book could be called a health book. Misunderstanding about nutritionally adequate and inadequate vegetarian meals is widespread. "Cooking With Conscience" attempts to throw some practical light on the subject. There is also the long term situation. The world really is running short of food for us as well as for everyone else. At best we face a period of serious adjustment. Our eating patterns are going to have to change. What is a matter of conscience today may very well be a matter of necessity tomorrow.

In the back of this book we have a bibliography of useful cookbooks, but I would like to mention here the groundbreaking work of Frances Moore Lappe, author of "Diet For A Small Planet" and her friend, Ellen Buchman Ewald, author of "Recipes For a Small Planet". Our book is much simpler and quite different, but without these two titles we would never have written "Cooking With Conscience". What they did was to take modern scientific research concerning vegetable protein and put it into usable form for the general public. And vegetable protein, as we will explain in the next section, is a vastly different matter than simply cooking vegetables in a tasty manner. It is a matter of complex nutritional balances between different foods, no one of which is a complete protein in itself. The world owes both authors a great debt.

Our book differs from theirs in several ways. First, it is not primarily concerned with the kind of foods we think of as Health foods. This is not that we don't believe in the value of natural, untreated foods nor in the ecological value of organic methods. (We have been organic gardeners for twenty and twenty-five years respectively.) But for the average cook the change over to cooking well balanced vegetable protein meals is complicated enough without calling for unusual ingredients not available in most markets. We therefore limited such ingredients to five (raw peanuts, sunflower kernels, unhulled sesame seeds, soy grits & bulgur) & have provided addresses where they may be ordered if not available locally.

In every way we could think of, our book was designed for those who are just beginning to cook vegetarian meals. The recipes were kept as simple as possible. For instance, although one can always substitute dried beans, we usually list canned beans instead. (If you have an old fashioned coal stove, and a large family, then cooking dried beans makes sense, but otherwise it uses a great deal of time and fuel when you have not yet discovered what your family likes.

But the major way in which we try to make it easy for the beginner is by making the meals seem as familiar as possible. Resistance to changed eating patterns is very strong. Even starving people sometimes refuse strange foods. Most of us were brought up to think that dinner means: meat, vegetable, and potato. Meals based on vegetable protein, milk and eggs often don't seem like dinner to us.

Luckily for Americans, the different peoples that have formed us have brought with them a wide variety of foods and cooking styles. One of us is old enough to remember when her mother brought broccoli from the Italian district of a New England city so that the family could have this "unusual" vegetable. What a vast change has come over American cooking since then! We may be eating more hamburger and steak than is good either for us or for the rest of the world, but we also probably have the most varied diet of any people, ever.

16

This varied diet makes possible a great number of dishes that either are familiar or seem familiar. I say "seem familiar" because they often have important changes in ingredients for nutritional reasons. This has sometimes slightly changed their taste and consistency. Sometimes a recipe may not be quite as delicious as one you are used to. But it will have much more protein.

Another difference between our book and those of Ewald and Lappe is that we are not as precisely scientific about nutritional needs. Instead, working from a scientific base, using their books and others, we have developed some simple rules of thumb for vegetable protein cooking and made these the basis for adapting familiar dishes and some less familiar ones that seemed appealing. We have also invented some quite new recipes, which we believe you will enjoy.

Besides the bibliography of cookbooks that we mentioned earlier, "Cooking With Conscience" contains a number of possibly useful sections in the back of the book. Immediately following this section is one on "Understanding Vegetable Protein", and unless you don't mind working completely in the dark, we recommend your reading it before you start cooking. Also, a prior reading of the section entitled "Please Read Before Cooking" may well save you later trouble or disappointment.

Although "Cooking With Conscience" was written for a serious purpose, we saw no reason to be glum about it. Cooking is a creative adventure and eating is a blessing. We enjoyed ourselves in putting this book together and we wish you enjoyment in using it.

Understanding Vegetable Protein

Most of us were brought up with a number of useful nutritional rules of thumb and a few stories to illustrate them, like Columbus's sailors getting scurvy because of a lack of fresh fruits and vegetables. But about protein, beyond the fact that we need it, we have remained relatively ignorant. Indeed, a great deal of the basic scientific work done on protein is of very recent origin.

Protein contains amino acids, eight of which are essential to health. Using egg as a protein norm, a vast number of foods have been tested as to their relative content of the essential eight (Isoleucine, Leucine, Lysine, Methionine, Phenylalanine, Threonine, Tryptophane and Valine). Certain foods were discovered to be high in protein but unfortunately not high in all the essential eight. Furthermore, in any given food the lowest amino acid on the score sheet was found to limit the nutritive value of the other seven. This has come to be called "the limiting amino acid," and it is of the utmost importance when considering the nutritive value of protein.

Fortunately, all foods are not low in the same amino acids, and when two or three foods containing the essential eight are combined in the proper proportion, the nutritive value of the protein increases--often quite dramatically. The essential principle to remember is: TO GET THE BEST USE OF ANY PROTEIN, THE EIGHT ESSENTIAL AMINO ACIDS SHOULD BE PRESENT, AND PRESENT IN THE RIGHT PROPORTION, IN THE SAME MEAL.

This is easier said than done. We sometimes departed from this principle (as little as possible) for matters of taste. But there is the more difficult task of learning a whole new system. "Diet for a Small Planet" and "Recipes for a Small Planet" have useful charts for the non-scientists, but even such simple charts turn out to be difficult to use when you get down to it. It is not merely a matter of understanding something when you look at it; the problem is that the whole language is unfamiliar, and when you turn away from the charts, you forget it and find yourself juggling amino acids, recipes, your family's tastes, and the number you plan to feed until you are dizzy.

Eventually we were able to absorb some simple rules of thumb for food combinations and based our recipes on these. In case you would like to strike out on your own, we have included an even more simplified chart for your guidance. The proportions are not precisely scientific, but they are a lot nearer than you are apt to get if you try to create a meatless meal without any guidelines at all. You don't have to know even these simplified rules of thumb if you use our menus, but we realize that at least some of you would like a basic understanding of the reasoning behind the recipes.

The most common combinations of foods that provide good balances of essential amino acids are: legumes and whole grains; whole grains and milk; legumes and seeds. Legumes, of course, means dried peas and beans and also includes peanuts. Whole grains means any whole grains such as wheat, rice, corn, barley, oats, etc. Milk means not only milk but cheese and yogurt. Seeds may include a lot of different seeds, but the only ones we have used are sunflower seed kernels and unhulled sesame seeds. One can also combine these foods in other fashions (see our chart) but the above combinations are the most common. One other pair shown on our chart is potatoes and milk.

To help you learn these combinations, you might remember such familiar ones as: bread and milk, beans and rice, and a peanut butter sandwich. Seeds are less usual in the American diet, but we wouldn't be surprised to learn that all of those spice seeds the Indians grind up in their curries don't help along the protein in their lentils and rice.

SOME SIMPLE RULES OF THUMB for combining meatless foods to produce more nutritionally usable protein:

1 PART LEGUMES and 2 PARTS MILK

2 PARTS LEGUMES and 3 PARTS SEEDS

1 PART LEGUMES and 3 PARTS WHOLE GRAINS

4 PARTS MILK and 3 PARTS WHOLE GRAINS

1 PART MILK (scant) and 1 PART SEEDS

1 PART MILK (scant) and 1 PART PEANUTS

1 PART MILK and 1 PART POTATO

Please note that the legumes, grains and seeds in this chart are in dry measure. In cooking, grains expand approximately by three, as do most legumes. Lentils and split peas approximately double in quantity when cooked. Also note that recipes calling for one part milk may substitute 1/3 as much cheese or instant powdered milk.

Very broad claims have been made lately about the protein value of soy beans. We agree that they are very high in protein and contain all of the essential amino acids. But soy beans alone are not sufficiently high in all of the essential eight to provide a nutritionally sound and economical source of protein. This could be remedied in cooking by using smaller amounts of soy beans (than other legumes) in proportion to grains, etc., if the culinary problem did not arise. We are just unused to large plates of rice with a few beans.

There is an easy solution to this problem, but we believe that it lies largely in the domain of the food industry. The meat extenders & textured vegetable proteins now on the market are usually produced from soy. Or if they contain other protein ingredients to make them a better substitute for meat than soy alone, they do not adequately explain this to the consumer. Soy flour is more easily used by cooks & in commercial products, but again, consumer education is lacking.

Many people are concerned about the high calorie content of meals containing so many carbohydrates. It is true that if you compare the calorie content of our recipes with the amount of meat needed to provide a similar amount of protein, the meat is usually lower in calories. Although we know of no complete study on the subject, it is comforting to realize that many people on a completely vegetarian diet report a weight loss rather than a weight gain. Perhaps this is because vegetable protein meals are very filling. You often need less than you expect. Also, in most meatless meals the cholesterol level drops tremendously. (You may substitute Eggbeaters for eggs in many of our recipes. Their protein level is high and of excellent quality, and we usually find them indistinguishable from eggs.) Another health factor to consider is the recent research showing that the American diet is in need of a great deal more fibre content such as is available in whole grains and legumes.

It may seem strange that in a vegetarian cookbook we have paid so little attention to those foods we normally think of as "vegetables." The importance of the vitamin content of fresh vegetables is well known, but most are quite low in protein. A few vegetables, however, should be mentioned. Mushrooms are quite high in protein and combine well nutritionally in the same meal with either cauliflower, broccoli, lima beans or spinach, which are high in other amino acids. Asparagus falls into the same category as mushrooms (although not as high in protein) and combines well nutritionally with any of the vegetables mentioned above. On the other hand, eggplant and sweet potato, which are delicious and filling, are disappointingly low in protein. But that doesn't mean that we should not eat them or any other vegetables. (Just don't count on their providing your needed protein.) The vitamin content of vegetables is so well known that it is superfluous to mention it, and the lighter texture and color contrast of a good salad or well cooked vegetables seem an even better contrast to grains, beans and eggs than they do to meat.

Please Read Before Cooking

Cooking a vegetarian meal is apt to take more time than you expect. Since this is an introductory book, we did everything we could to lessen the time needed for cooking and preparation. For instance, cooking dry beans is a slow process, sometimes taking hours, and therefore we frequently suggest using canned beans. (Later in this section we suggest various cooking methods for dry beans if you wish to use them.) Many of our menus can be prepared quickly, but in others the procedures are unfamiliar, and this slows you down at first. Also, many recipes call for an unusual amount of chopping, slicing or blending. For this we have no easy answer other than providing yourselves with good knives, choppers, and graters. A blender is very useful, and a food mill an inexpensive substitute. But we have also found that in these days of instant foods and hectic lives, chopping vegetables in the kitchen can be a very peaceful and restorative occupation.

If you are just introducing your family to vegetarian food, choose your first menu with care! Young adults are usually very open to the idea, but children often don't like strange or spicy foods. Menus Two, Three, Thirty-one, Thirty-eight, and Forty-three are apt to be liked by children. Also, our wonderful Crunchy Whole Wheat Bread (Menu Eight) is packed with protein and any simple cream soup and a few carrot sticks, should make a pleasing meal for both young and old. It is also wise, and not only for nutritional reasons, to include all of the foods in a menu that we say are needed for protein. In our experience, if you leave any out, appetites will not be satisfied.

A few words of caution on measuring are in order. On our chart we used dry measures of beans and grain. In our recipes we sometimes call for dry measures and sometimes call for cooked measures. Please read carefully. We did this for several reasons: It is usually easier to start a dish with cooked canned beans, or rice you've cooked the day before, (or perhaps had in your freezer). On the other hand, with quick cooking split peas and lentils (read before you buy!) cooking times are not excessive, so we are apt to call for dry measures. But when I came to the chart we felt that we had to be consistent and used uncooked measures. A similar confusion can be made when we call for powdered milk. We really mean the powder and never mean reconstituted powdered milk. (1/3 of a cup of instant powdered milk has the protein in 1 cup of whole milk, takes less room and has less cholesterol.)

As stated earlier we have only called for five ingredients not readily available in most markets. We often call for soy grits because a few can be added, when needed nutritionally, without changing the taste of a dish greatly. They are as high in protein as soy beans, but do not need long cooking. We have called for raw peanuts, not only because they are delicious but because they are unsalted. Be sure to ask for ones without the paper skins as it saves trouble. Sunflower kernels are the seeds with the hard outer covering removed. But sesame seeds lose nutrients and flavor if hulled. (Don't buy the expensive hulled ones sold in small jars.) Bulgur is available in some markets. It is whole wheat prepared for easy cooking.

Cooking times and methods of all beans, peas and lentils vary wildly. Some quick-cooking split peas and lentils can be put in twice the measure of boiling water, and they are done in 20 to 30 minutes. Some take longer. Red kidney beans can sometimes be cooked in 30 minutes (if first soaked over night), but sometimes take 2 hours. Most varieties take 1 or 2 hours (after soaking all night) but garbanzos and soy beans can take up to 4 hours! It all depends on the brand, their age, the humidity and goodness knows what else. "Recipes for a Small Planet" suggests that you shorten cooking times by pressure cooking. Freezing soaked beans before cooking also shortens the time. Personally, we find the easiest way is to soak a pound box overnight in 7 cups of water. Then add

3 more cups of water and put on to simmer in a large pot on some day when you are puttering around the house. Take a look once in a while, stir, add more water if needed, and take off the stove when they taste done. Then cool them and freeze in measured packages for later use. (Never add baking soda -- it destroys a number of B vitamins.)

While on the subject of beans we should say that the varieties available (both canned and dry) vary from one part of the country to the other. Kidney beans are in pretty wide supply so we suggest them often, but you may substitute. (Chick peas and garbanzos are different names for the same thing.)

Brown rice can also be cooked in quantity and frozen. It takes about 45 minutes to boil, and an excellent way to cook it is in a double boiler. Use 2 cups of water to 1 cup of rice and 1 t salt. Cook covered, over boiling water, about 50 minutes or until water is absorbed.

A word on curry powder would not be amiss. The less expensive kinds are usually extra mild, but when we say "mild curry powder" what we mean is: don't use a kind that says it is "hot". At least don't unless you love hot curry.

With that last warning, we leave you on your own and wish you good cooking.

52

MENUS

One

This sounds most unlikely, but if you feel adventurous, try it. All nuts are an excellent source of protein, and unlike peanuts, which are legumes, they help to complete the protein in beans, peas, and, for that matter, in peanuts. But since nuts are expensive, this is our only recipe that calls for them. Serve the spaghetti with a fresh spinach salad, Italian bread, and our own garlic spread.
SERVES 3 OR 4

Spaghetti with Walnuts and Lentils

1/2 cup lentils
1 cup chopped walnut
        meats
1/4 t garlic powder
1/2 cup olive oil
1/2 cup vegetable oil
1/3 cup unhulled sesame
        seeds
1 T parsley
1/4 cup wheat germ
3/4 cup Parmesan cheese,
        grated
1 lb. spaghetti

Cook lentils according to directions on the package. Drain. Mix lentils, walnuts, garlic, oils, seeds and parsley. Warm but do not cook. Boil spaghetti according to directions on package. Drain. Mix with sauce & then with wheat germ and cheese. Serve immediately.

Garlic Spread

1 stick butter or
        margarine
1/4 t garlic powder
1 T chopped parsley
4 T powdered milk
1 T vegetable oil

Mix and let stand one hour at room temperature.

Two

Anyone who has been to Ireland knows that the Irish know how to cook potatoes to perfection. This is obviously not an Irish recipe, but my introduction to potato pancakes was through an Irish friend. A green vegetable completes the meal.
SERVES 3 OR 4

Bridget's Potato Pancakes

3 large potatoes
1 onion, finely
        chopped
1 egg
1 cup powdered milk
1/4 cup flour
2 t baking powder
1/2 t salt
1/8 t pepper
1/2 cup water
3 T butter or margarine
3 T vegetable oil

Scrub potatoes well and cut out any bad spots. Peel if desired. Grate with a very coarse grater or a shredder. Put butter & oil in a frying pan. Mix potatoes in bowl with all other ingredients and fry by spoonfuls until brown on both sides.

Scalloped Tomatoes

2 cans (16 oz.) stewed
        tomatoes
1 cup herb stuffing
1/4 cup wheat germ
1/4 cup soy grits
1/3 cup vegetable oil
1/2 t salt
1/4 t pepper

Strain tomatoes, reserving liquid in a bowl. Mix tomato liquid and all other ingredients. Put 1/2 the tomatoes in a greased casserole. Top with 1/2 the stuffing mixture & then with the remaining tomatoes. Finish off with the remaining stuffing mixture. Bake for 45 minutes in a 350 degree oven.

Three

More years ago than we would like to remember, one of us was a
student living in a boarding house. The cook's name was Mary,
and she introduced me to an egg dish that has become a tradition
in our family.
SERVES 2 OR 3

Mary's Eggs

4 eggs
4 slices whole wheat
    bread
1 can condensed tomato
    soup
1 t Lea & Perrin's
    Worcestershire
    sauce
1 dash Tabasco
2 T margarine

Cut circles (2-1/2" wide) out of
each piece of bread with a cookie
cutter or glass. Fry bread until brown on one side in margarine in a large frying pan. Turn
bread and break an egg into each
hole. Sprinkle with salt and
pepper. Cover pan and cook
over medium heat until whites
are just set. Meanwhile, heat
condensed soup with Tabasco &
Worcestershire sauces. Pour
this sauce over eggs and serve.
(The bread circles should also
be browned and served.)

Peanut Coleslaw

2 cups shredded cabbage
1/2 cup raw peanuts,
    chopped
2 grated carrots
1/2 cup mayonnaise or
    more to taste
1 T lemon juice
1 t celery seeds

Shred, chop, grate, mix, and
serve.

Four

Served with yellow squash sprinkled with 1/3 cup unhulled sesame seeds, this makes a delicious and balanced meal.
SERVES 3 OR 4

Whole Wheat Crust

1 cup whole wheat
        pastry flour
1/4 t salt
1/4 cup vegetable oil
1/8 cup ice water

Add salt to the flour. Blend the oil in with a fork. Add ice water, a T at a time. Mix well after each addition. Shape into a ball and roll out with floured rolling pin on a floured surface into a circle 1" larger than pie pan. Fit into pan and flute edge so that it stands up.

Broccoli Quiche

1-1/2 cups chopped
        broccoli
1/2 cup boiling water
2 T chopped onion
1 T oil
4 eggs
2 cups milk
1/2 t salt
1/4 t pepper
1/2 t mustard
1/4 cup Parmesan
        cheese, grated
1/4 cup Swiss cheese,
        grated

Cut off thick stems of broccoli. Peel & chop in smaller pieces than the rest. Put broccoli (larger pieces on bottom) into a pan with 1/2 cup boiling water. Simmer until just tender. Drain well. Saute onion in oil until tender. Put milk, eggs, salt, pepper & mustard into a bowl & beat well. Fill pie shell with broccoli, onion & cheese. Pour egg mixture over it and bake for 15 minutes in oven preheated to 450 degrees. Reduce to 350 degrees & bake about 10 minutes longer or until knife inserted in center comes out clean.

Five

There is nothing in this meal that has the appearance of meat, but it is simple, good, filling, and well supplied with protein. Serve with a green salad.
SERVES 2 OR 3

Eastern Pilaf

2 cups cooked brown
    rice
3 T seedless raisins
1/4 cup water
1/4 cup raw peanuts,
    chopped
2 medium onions,
    sliced
2 T butter or margarine
1/2 t salt

Soak raisins one hour or more in water. Slice onions & fry in butter until brown. Mix all ingredients and heat in a double boiler. Bulgur or other whole grains may be substituted.

Creamed Carrots with Wheat Germ

7 or 8 carrots
1 cup milk
1/3 cup powdered milk
1 t parsley
1 t salt
1/2 t pepper
4 T butter or margarine
2 T flour
1/4 cup wheat germ

Steam or boil carrots until just tender. Bring milk, powdered milk, and 2 T butter to a simmer in a saucepan. Put flour in a bowl and add hot milk slowly while beating with a wire whisk. Return to saucepan and bring to a boil while stirring. Remove from heat and add salt, pepper, carrots and parsley. Reheat if needed. Melt the remaining 2 T butter in a small pan, add wheat germ, mix, and sprinkle on carrots before serving.

Six

Soy sauce (when it is really made from soy beans) and rice form a good protein combination, but this meal will provide a better one. SERVES 4 OR 5

Chinese Sweet and Sour

1 green pepper
2 onions, sliced
2 T vegetable oil
1 (16 oz.) can bean
    sprouts
1 (16 oz.) can kidney
    beans
1 (8 oz.) can crushed
    pineapple
2 T cornstarch
1/4 cup soy sauce
1 t salt
1/3 cup brown sugar
1/4 cup cider vinegar
1/3 cup sunflower
    kernels

Core pepper & cut in thin strips. Fry onion & pepper in oil until just tender. Drain liquid from bean sprouts and discard. Drain liquid from kidney beans and pineapple into a saucepan. Add cornstarch and beat smooth with wire whisk. Add sugar, salt, vinegar and soy sauce. Bring to a boil while stirring. Reduce to a simmer and add other ingredients. Mix, heat, and serve.

Fried Rice

4 cups cold, cooked
    brown rice
1 carrot
1 bunch scallions
4 T vegetable oil
2 T Kikkoman soy sauce
2 beaten eggs
1 t salt

Chop carrot finely. Chop scallions including about an inch of the green. Cook carrot & scallions in oil in large frying pan until golden. Add rice and soy sauce. Stir and fry for 2 or 3 minutes longer. Stir in the beaten eggs and salt. Stir and cook 3 minutes more.

34

Seven

This is fun, simple and good. Serve with a good soy sauce and brown rice which are needed to help complete the protein and green peas.
SERVES 5 OR 6

Eggs Foo Yung

6 eggs
1 can (16 oz.) bean
        sprouts
2 medium onions, finely
        chopped
2 T soy sauce
1/2 t salt
1 cup finely chopped
        fresh mushrooms
1/4 cup chopped fresh
        parsley
vegetable oil

Beat eggs slightly in a large bowl. Add other ingredients and mix well. Fry pancakes of the mixture in oil until brown.

Eight

Aside from the delight of smelling and eating home-baked bread, we have included this recipe because it is rich in protein and has an unusually delicious taste and texture. Serve with any soup.
3 LOAVES (1 lb. pans)

Crunchy Whole Wheat Bread

3 packages yeast
1 T brown sugar
1 cup lukewarm water
        ****
3 cups lukewarm water
3 T brown sugar
2 T salt
1 cup powdered milk
1/2 cup vegetable oil
        ****
3 cups whole wheat
        flour
        ****
1 cup wheat germ
3 cups white flour
2 cups whole wheat
        flour
        ****

Combine first 3 ingredients in a small bowl, stir and set aside. Combine next 5 ingredients in a large bowl & stir. Add yeast mixture & 3 cups whole wheat flour and beat until smooth. Add wheat germ and remaining flour, a cup at a time, beating until smooth. This will take a strong arm, but it's worth it, and there is no kneading to be done. Cover bowl with damp towel and set in warm place (around 85 degrees) until doubled in size. Spoon into 3 greased bread pans and smooth down a bit. (The dough will be sticky.) Cover with damp towel and let rise until doubled in size. (The rising times each take about 1 hour but vary widely with the temperature. Never use a hot place, it kills the yeast; but very slow rising is fine.) Bake in preheated 350 degree oven for 40-50 minutes. Bread is done when it shrinks away from side of pan. Turn out on rack. Brush with melted butter. Cool before slicing.

Nine

Here are two soups to go with the bread on the opposite page. A fruit salad goes well with the bread and either soup.
SERVES 5

Black Bean Soup

2 cups dry black beans
2 qts water (plus
     soaking water)
2 T bacon fat (or
     vegetable oil)
1 large onion, sliced
2 carrots, sliced
3 stalks celery, sliced
3 cloves stuck into a
     small onion
2 bay leaves
2 t salt
1/2 t pepper
1/2 t dry mustard
1 lemon
1 hard boiled egg
sherry (optional)

Soak beans overnight in 7 cups water. Cook onion until soft in bacon fat or oil. Put all ingredients, except last 3, in a large pot. Bring to a boil, reduce heat and simmer 3 hours or until beans are soft. Remove cloves and bayleaves & put all ingredients except lemon, egg and sherry in blender (a cup or so at a time) & blend smooth or force through food mill. Return to pot and reheat. To each bowl of soup add 1 T sherry, 1 slice hard boiled egg and 1 thin slice of lemon.

Pureé Mongole

1-1/2 cups split peas
     (quick cooking)
6 cups water
2 cans condensed
     tomato soup
2 onions, chopped
3 T butter or margarine
1 t salt
1/2 t pepper
2 t mild curry powder
4 T sherry (optional)

Put peas & water in a pot. Bring to a boil and reduce heat. Simmer 30 minutes or until peas are soft. Cook onion in butter until soft. When peas are done, add all other ingredients, stir well, heat and serve.

Ten

A simple, unpretentious meal. Serve with any creamed vegetable.
SERVES 3 OR 4

Simple Bulgur

4 T butter or margarine
1-1/2 cups bulgur
2 medium onions,
        chopped
1 t salt
3 cups water
2 T parsley

Melt butter in a large frying pan. Add onions and bulgur and stir and fry for 5 minutes. Drain & measure the water from the can of chick peas that you will use in the salad. Add enough water to make 3 cups and add to the frying pan. Bring to a simmer, cover, and simmer 20 minutes. Add parsley and serve.

Chick Pea Salad

1 can (16 oz.) chick
        peas
1/2 cup unhulled sesame
        seeds
1 medium onion, chopped
2 carrots, chopped
1/4 cup vegetable oil
1/4 cup cider vinegar
1 T sugar
1 t salt
1/2 t medium grind
        pepper
1/4 cup fresh chives,
        chopped
1 tomato

Drain the chick peas and mix in a bowl with all the other ingredients except the tomato and chives. Cover the bowl & chill 2 hours or overnight. Cut the tomato in small pieces, mix in along with the chives.

Eleven

One of our most pleasant discoveries was the nutritional value of sunflower seed kernels.
SERVES 3 OR 4

Sunflower Salad

1/4 cup fresh parsley
1 medium onion
2 carrots
1 t dry mustard
1/2 t pepper
1 t salt
1/3 cup olive oil
2 T vinegar
3 cups cooked brown
     rice
1/4 cup soy grits
1/2 cup sunflower
     kernels

Mince parsley and onion.
Grate carrots coarsely. Mix
oil, vinegar, mustard, salt,
and pepper in a good sized bowl.
Add other ingredients, mix, and
serve.

Spinach Au Gratin

2 packages frozen
     chopped spinach
     (or use fresh
     spinach)
1/2 t salt
1/2 cup milk
1/3 cup powdered milk
2 T flour
2 T butter or margarine
1/4 cup wheat germ
1/2 cup grated Parmesan
     cheese

Defrost spinach. Place in
saucepan in 1/2 cup water and
stir with a fork. Bring to a boil,
reduce heat and simmer, covered, for 4 minutes. Add butter and remove from heat. In
small bowl mix flour, salt, milk
and powdered milk with a wire
whisk. Add to saucepan and
stir over medium high heat until mixture thickens. Place in
buttered casserole. Sprinkle
with cheese and wheat germ and
bake in a 350 degree oven for
30 minutes.

Twelve

These crepes are easy to make. Spoon the creamed mushrooms onto each crepe. Roll them and top with another spoonful of the mushrooms. Any green vegetable will complete the meal.
SERVES 2

Whole Wheat Crepes

1 cup milk
2 eggs
1/2 t salt
2 T oil
1 cup whole wheat flour

Blend or beat milk, eggs, salt & oil. Beat in flour until smooth, scraping sides of bowl. Let stand 30 minutes. Beat again. Heat a 6-7" frying pan & grease lightly with oil. Pour 1/4 cup batter into pan tilting to cover bottom. Cook for about 1 minute. Flip & cook 1/2 minute. Renew oil as needed. Set a saucepan 1/2 full of water on to simmer. Place plate on top and as crepes are cooked stack on plate. Keep lightly covered with foil.

Creamed Mushrooms

1 lb. fresh mushrooms,
    chopped
4 T butter or margarine
4 T flour
1-1/3 cups milk
1/2 cup powdered milk
1/2 t salt
1 T sherry (optional)
1 T chopped parsley

Brown mushrooms in butter over high heat, shaking pan constantly. Reduce heat, stir in seasonings and half the milk. Put flour & rest of milk & powdered milk in small bowl & beat until smooth with wire whisk. Add milk and flour mixture slowly to pan, stirring constantly until thickened. Add sherry. Heat but do not boil.

Thirteen

If you use a cornbread mix make sure it contains milk. (Our own cornbread recipe is in menu forty-one.) This is a quick and easy meal to prepare. If only serving 2, use 1/2 as much cornbread but serve milk with the meal for the protein balance.
SERVES 2 OR 3

Chili with Cornbread Topping

1 medium onion, chopped
1 clove garlic, minced
2 T oil
1 can (16 oz.) kidney
    beans
1 can (16 oz.) stewed
    tomatoes
1/2 cup sunflower
    kernels
2 T chili powder
1-1/2 t salt
1/2 t celery seed
1 package cornbread mix

Fry onions and garlic in oil in a large frying pan until soft. Add all other ingredients except corn bread. Mix, and simmer until thick. (About 1/2 hour). Preheat oven to temperature suggested on cornbread package. Mix batter, and drop by spoonfuls on warm chili. (If your frying pan is all metal, it may also double as your baking pan. Otherwise, use a casserole.) Bake as directed for cornbread.

Salad without Lettuce

1 cup or more leftover
    cooked green vege-
    tables such as
    beans, peas, or
    broccoli
1 cup or more chopped
    or sliced crunchy,
    raw vegetables such
    as celery, carrots,
    green peppers, and
    radishes
1/4 cup French dressing
1/4 cup plain yogurt

Chop, slice, mix, and serve.

Fourteen

Gazpacho, the Spanish tomato soup that is served cold, is both simple and delicious. But you really need a blender. If you don't have one, borrow a neighbor's and ask them to dinner some hot summer night.
SERVES 4 OR 5

Gazpacho

2 cups V-8 juice
1/2 cup olive oil
4 eggs
1/2 cup vinegar
2 green peppers
2 small onions, peeled
6 fresh tomatoes
3 peeled cucumbers
1/4 t salt
1/4 t Lea & Perrins
    Worcestershire
    sauce
2 cloves of garlic

Chop finely 1/2 a green pepper, 1 cucumber & 1 onion. Put in separate serving dishes, cover & chill. Put croutons in another & place out of reach of nibblers. Cut remaining vegetables into pieces. Put liquid ingredients and seasonings in blender. Blend vegetables, a few at a time, until liquid. When all is liquid, cover & chill. Serve with dishes of croutons and chopped vegetables.

Raisin Bran Muffins

1-1/2 cups whole wheat
    flour
3 t baking powder
1 t salt
1/2 cup brown sugar
    (or molasses)
1-1/2 cups bran cereal
1 cup milk
1 egg
1/3 cup vegetable oil
1/2 cup raisins
1/3 cup raw peanuts,
    chopped

Sift together flour, baking powder & salt. Combine bran and milk. Let stand until moisture is absorbed. Add egg, sugar & oil and beat well. Add dry ingredients, stirring only until combined. Stir in raisins and peanuts and fill greased muffin cups 3/4 full. Bake about 15 minutes in oven preheated to 400 degrees.

Fifteen

Tortillas for tacos can be found in grocery stores in the freezer or on the shelf. Steam them to soften as it makes them easier to fill and eat. (Or fry until crisp, if preferred.) The salad is not needed for protein but makes a good accompaniment.
SERVES 2

Tacos with Bean Filling

1 can (16 oz.) red
    kidney beans
1 medium onion, chopped
2 T vegetable oil
1 T chili powder
1/4 t garlic powder
1/4 cup catsup or
    barbecue sauce
1/4 t oregano
1/2 cup shredded cheese
4 corn tortillas

Drain beans, reserving liquid. In a 2 qt. saucepan saute onion in oil until tender. Add 1 cup beans & mash. Add remaining beans. Stir in chili powder, garlic powder, oregano & catsup or barbecue sauce. While stirring, bring to a boil then reduce heat & let simmer for 5-10 minutes. This mixture should be thick, but if too thick, thin with the bean liquid. (This would taste better if made the day before so that flavors can blend.) To serve, spoon bean mixture into folded, steamed tacos and top with cheese.

Grapefruit and Avocado Salad

1 grapefruit
1 ripe avocado
1 stalk celery, sliced
6 radishes, sliced
lettuce
Italian dressing

Peel and remove sections from grapefruit, making sure no white inner peel remains. Cut each section in half. Peel & remove pit from avocado and cut into chunks. Mix in celery and radishes. Toss with dressing and serve on bed of lettuce.

43

Sixteen

Here's a meal for a crowd. Add bread and it will go even further. Delicious, filling, and nutritious.
SERVES 10

Lasagna

1 package lasagna
    noodles (1 lb.)
1 medium onion, chopped
2 T vegetable oil
4 cups marinara sauce
1/2 cup soy grits
1/2 cup wheat germ
1 lb. Ricotta or cot-
    tage cheese
1 lb. Mozzarella cheese
    cut in slivers
2 eggs
1 cup grated Parmesan
    cheese
1/2 t salt
1/4 t pepper

Boil lasagna according to package directions. Fry onion in oil until golden and add to marinara sauce. Stir in soy grits and wheat germ. Mix cheeses, eggs, salt and pepper. Put thin layer of tomato sauce in greased casserole. Add a layer of lasagna, a layer of cheese and more sauce. Repeat until finished, ending with cheese. Bake covered at 325 degrees for 30 minutes. Remove cover and bake for 15 minutes more.

Three Bean Salad

1 can (16 oz.) EACH
    green beans
    garbanzos
    kidney beans
1 green pepper, chopped
2 medium onions,
    chopped
2 cups chopped celery
1/2 cup chopped parsley
2 t salt
2 T sugar
1/2 t pepper
1/4 cup vinegar
1/2 cup vegetable oil

Drain beans and save liquid for a soup. Mix with other ingredients and serve. Will taste much better if made in advance.

Seventeen

Welsh rarebit is a simple, old favorite. If you prefer your own recipe, use it. Just make sure that the toast is a whole wheat or another whole grain toast. Although green beans are high in protein, they are not essential for this meal--but the peanuts are necessary.
SERVES 3 OR 4

Welsh Rarebit on Whole Wheat Toast

1/2 lb. sharp cheddar, grated
1 T butter
1/4 t salt
1/2 t dry mustard
1/2 t Lea & Perrin's Worcestershire sauce
1/2 cup milk
8 or more slices whole wheat toast

Heat milk in a double boiler. When hot add other ingredients. Heat until cheese is melted, stirring occasionally with a wire whisk. Serve over whole wheat toast.

Green Beans with Peanuts

2 boxes frozen green beans (or equivalent in fresh)
1/3 cup raw peanuts
2 T butter or margarine

Steam or boil the beans. Melt the butter. Chop peanuts fairly fine and mix with butter. Pour over cooked beans.

Eighteen

If you are used to thinking of French Toast as something with maple syrup for breakfast, this menu and the next may sound a bit startling, but the taste combination is simple and good. Serve with any green vegetable.
SERVES 5 OR 6

Lima Bean and Onion Filling

1 can (16 oz.) big
        white lima beans
        (or other white
        beans)
2 medium onions, chopped
1/2 green pepper,
        chopped
3 T vegetable oil
1 T parsley
1 t salt
1 t paprika
1/8 t cayenne

Cook onion and pepper in oil until soft. Drain beans. (Save the liquid for a soup.) Mash the beans, a few at a time, on a plate with a fork. Put them in a bowl with the other ingredients and mix well.

French Toast with Tomato Sauce

16 slices whole wheat
        bread
3 eggs
1 t salt
1 cup milk
3 T butter or margarine
2 cans condensed tomato
        soup
1 cup grated cheese
1 t Lea and Perrins
        Worcestershire
        sauce

Spread the filling on 8 slices of bread and top with the other slices. Press down lightly and cut each sandwich in three long pieces. Beat eggs with milk and salt. Dip sandwiches in this mixture and brown on both sides in butter. Heat condensed soup, cheese, and Worcestershire sauce and serve as a sauce.

Nineteen

Use the recipe for French Toast on facing page, but use Bean and Peanut Filling and serve with Mild Curry Sauce.
SERVES 4 OR 5

Bean and Peanut Filling

1 can (16 oz.) kidney
        beans
1 medium onion, chopped
2 T vegetable oil
1/2 cup raw peanuts,
        chopped
1 t salt
1/4 t pepper

Cook onion in oil until soft. Drain beans and mash on a plate with a fork. Put all ingredients in a bowl and mix well.

Mild Curry Sauce

3 T butter or margarine
3 T flour
1-1/2 cups milk
1/2 cup powdered milk
1-1/2 t lemon juice
1-1/2 T mild curry
        powder
1/2 t salt
1/8 t pepper
2 t minced onion (dried
        or fresh)

Melt butter in a saucepan. Mix in flour with a wire whisk. Slowly add the milk while stirring over medium heat until the sauce thickens and comes to a boil. Remove from heat & stir in powdered milk and other ingredients. Return to heat and cook and stir one minute more.

Twenty

People don't ordinarily think of potatoes as having protein, but they do, and milk or cheese help to complete the protein.
SERVES 4

Eggplant and Cheese Casserole

1/2 cup herb stuffing
1/4 cup wheat germ
1/2 cup milk
3 eggs
1 t salt
1/4 t paprika
1/2 t thyme
1 large eggplant
1/4 cup vegetable oil
1 cup grated cheese

Mix herb stuffing, milk, eggs, wheat germ and seasonings in a large bowl. Peel and slice eggplant. Place on shallow baking pan and sprinkle with oil. Broil on both sides until slightly brown. Then add to mixture in bowl. Mix well, breaking eggplant into slightly smaller pieces. Put in greased casserole, top with cheese and bake 1 hour at 325 degrees.

Baked Potatoes and Sour Cream

4 baking potatoes
1/2 pint sour cream

Put potatoes in oven 1/2 hour before you put the casserole in.

Sesame Salad

1/2 cup unhulled sesame
    seeds
1 can (16 oz.) kidney
    beans
assorted greens
French or Italian
    dressing

The important ingredients for protein, of course, are the beans and seeds. Mix all ingredients and serve.

Twenty-one

These are two very simple dishes but they are also unusually good.
SERVES 6 OR 8

New Orleans Beans and Rice

3 cups raw brown rice
5 cups water
2 medium onions, chopped
2 green peppers
2 T vegetable oil
1 can (16 oz.) kidney
    beans
1 bay leaf
1 t salt
1/2 t pepper
1/3 cup Bacos
1/2 cup olive oil
3 T vinegar
2 additional onions,
    chopped

Put rice and water in a large saucepan or Dutch oven. Bring to a boil, reduce heat and simmer 30 minutes. Core green pepper and chop. Cook pepper and onion in oil until soft and add to cooked rice with beans, bay leaf, salt, and pepper. Mix and simmer 20 more minutes. Add all other ingredients except the 2 chopped onions. Mix and heat. Serve with chopped onions sprinkled on top.

Robert's Cucumbers

6 cucumbers
1 T salt
1 t chopped dill weed
1/8 t garlic powder
1/2 cup yogurt

Peel and slice cucumbers the night before serving. Layer in large bowl sprinkling each layer lightly with salt. Refrigerate until shortly before serving. Pour off water. Mix in dill and yogurt and garlic powder.

Twenty-two

We couldn't resist having one dish called "A Mess of Pottage".
According to some Biblical translations, Esau sold his birthright
to his brother Jacob for "a mess of pottage". Other translations
say "bread and lentiles" and still others say "bread and lentil
soup". In any case, it was lentils and probably cooked with onions,
butter, and a few herbs. Who knows?--this might even be some-
where close to the original. (Except those were red lentils, and
brown ones are easier for us to find. And he certainly didn't add
powdered milk.) Serve with any whole grain bread to help complete
the protein and a plate of raw vegetables such as carrot sticks and
celery.
SERVES 3 OR 4

A Mess of Pottage

1 cup lentils
3 large onions, chopped
1 clove garlic,
       minced
1/2 stick butter or
       margarine
1 t cumin powder
3 T parsley
2 t salt
1/2 t paprika
3/4 cup powdered milk

Put lentils in a large pot with a
quart of water. Bring to a boil
and turn down to a simmer.
Meanwhile, cook onions and garlic in butter until golden and add
them and all other ingredients,
except the milk, to the soup.
Cook until lentils are tender and
stir in powdered milk.

Twenty-three

The soup is about as simple as you can make. The Hummus, a
Middle Eastern specialty, takes some time and trouble but is
worth it. Serve with celery and carrot sticks and brown-and-
serve French bread or flat Arabian bread, if your grocery has it.
SERVES 2

Cheese Soup with Fresh Tomatoes

1/2 green pepper
2 carrots
2 T butter or margarine
2 T flour
2 cups water
1/2 t salt
1/2 t Lea & Perrins
1-1/2 cups grated
       cheddar
2 fresh tomatoes,
       chopped

Chop green pepper and carrots &
saute in butter for 4 minutes.
Then simmer in water until soft.
Put flour in bowl and mix in some
of the hot liquid with a wire whisk.
Return mixture to pan and cook &
stir over medium heat until
smooth and thick. Add seasonings and cheese and stir until
melted. Mix in tomatoes shortly
before serving.

Hummus with Sesame Seeds

1/2 cup unhulled sesame
       seeds
2 T olive or vegetable
       oil
1 can (16 oz.) gar-
       banzos
2 cloves garlic, sliced
1/4 cup lemon juice
1 t salt
1/4 cup olive or vege-
       table oil
1 T parsley

Toast sesame seeds on a flat pan
in a 350 degree oven for 10 minutes. Put in blender and blend
until they become a powdery
paste. Add 2 T oil & blend 10
seconds. Drain garbanzos, sav-
ing liquid. Add remaining ingredients, except parsley. Blend,
stopping frequently to push mixture back down to blades with a
rubber scraper. Gradually add
enough bean liquid & blend to the
consistency of thick mashed potatoes. Add parsley. Cover &
chill. Return to room temperature before serving.

Twenty-four

A very simple and satisfying meal. The casserole may be prepared ahead of time.
SERVES 4 OR 5

Corn and Tomato Casserole

```
1 green pepper
2 T butter or margarine
1/3 cup vegetable oil
1 t salt
1/4 cup wheat germ
3/4 cup herb stuffing
1 can (16 oz.) cream
        style corn
1 can (16 oz.) tomatoes
1/4 cup soy grits
1/2 t pepper
1/2 cup grated cheese
```

Core and chop green pepper and brown in butter in a frying pan. Remove to a bowl with a slotted spoon. Add oil, salt, wheat germ and stuffing to frying pan and mix. Add corn, tomatoes, soy grits and pepper to bowl and mix. Put 1/2 stuffing mixture in bottom of a greased casserole and then pour in vegetables and top with the rest of the stuffing mixture and sprinkle with cheese. Bake in a 325 degree oven one hour.

Swiss Cheese Salad

```
1/4 lb. Swiss cheese
3 hard boiled eggs
lettuce and/or other
        salad greens
1/4 cup unhulled sesame
        seeds
1/3 cup yogurt
1/2 t dry mustard
1/2 t salt
1/2 t pepper
1/4 t cumin seeds (or
        1/2 t celery
        seeds)
1 t prepared horse-
        radish
```

Cut cheese in thin strips. Chop eggs in small pieces. Break up salad greens. Put them all in a salad bowl and add seeds. Mix other ingredients in a small bowl, then pour on the salad and toss well.

Twenty-five

You may use garbanzos or any other cooked or canned beans for this. Also, the salad may have any other ingredients, as long as the seeds and yogurt are included. Serve with squash, carrots, or parsnips. The croquettes may be served with the curry sauce in Menu Nineteen.
SERVES 3 OR 4

Bean Croquettes

1 can (16 oz.)
     garbanzos
1/2 cup powdered milk
1/2 cup wheat germ
1/4 t garlic powder
1 egg
1/4 t pepper
1/8 t cayenne
1/2 t salt
1/2 t curry powder
flour
1/4 vegetable oil

Drain garbanzos, reserving liquid. Mix egg and spices in a large bowl. Add garbanzos, milk, wheat germ and spices. Crush, and mix. (It doesn't need to be smooth.) Add bean liquid, if needed, for mixture to hold its shape. Form into croquettes (oblong patties) and chill. Roll in flour and fry in vegetable oil until brown.

Seed Salad

2 fresh tomatoes,
     chopped
1 cucumber, peeled and
     chopped
1/2 green pepper,
     chopped
1/2 cup minced fresh
     parsley
1/4 cup sunflower
     kernels
1/4 cup unhulled sesame
     seeds
1/4 cup yogurt
1/4 cup French or
     Italian dressing

Mix, toss, and serve.

Twenty-six

Serve this with yellow squash sprinkled with sesame seed.
SERVES 2

Top-of-the-Stove Garbanzo Casserole

```
1 can (16 oz.) gar-
    banzos
1 can (16 oz.) stewed
    tomatoes
2 carrots, sliced
2 medium onions, sliced
1 clove garlic, minced
2 T vegetable oil
1/4 cup wheat germ
1 t salt
1/2 t pepper
1 t basil
```

Fry onions and garlic in oil in large frying pan or Dutch oven until golden. Drain garbanzos and save liquid for a soup. Add all other ingredients and simmer uncovered for 30 minutes.

Winter or Summer Salad

```
1-1/2 cups cooked brown
    rice
4 T vegetable oil
2 T vinegar
1/2 t salt
1/4 t pepper
1/2 cup sunflower
    kernels
1 medium onion, minced
1/4 cup chopped fresh
    parsley
1/2 cup leftover cooked
    green vegetables
1/2 cup diced raw mush-
    rooms (or 1/2 cup
    diced fresh
    tomato)
```

Obviously, the "Winter or Summer" title comes from the choice between mushrooms (cheaper and better in the winter) and tomatoes (cheaper and better in the summer). Prepare your ingredients, mix and serve.

Twenty-seven

This is an excellent recipe to try with Eggbeaters instead of eggs, if you wish. Since the spinach is in the omelet, the two dishes make a complete meal, although you might wish to add sliced tomatoes.
SERVES 2

Spinach Omelet

1 package frozen
       chopped spinach
2 medium onions, sliced
2 T vegetable oil
4 beaten eggs
1/2 t salt
1/4 t pepper
1/8 t nutmeg
1/3 cup grated Parmesan
       cheese
2 T butter or margarine

Defrost spinach and cook according to package directions. Drain well. Cook onions in oil until golden. Add onions & seasonings to beaten eggs. Heat skillet over medium high heat. Melt butter and then add egg mixture. Lift edges with a spatula to allow uncooked eggs to run underneath. Sprinkle cheese on top while cooking. When fairly dry on top, increase heat a bit to brown. Fold in half and serve.

Creamed Potatoes

1 cup milk
2 T flour
2 T butter or margarine
1/4 t salt
1/8 t pepper
1/3 cup powdered milk
2 cups cold, boiled, &
       diced potatoes

Melt butter in the top of a double boiler over boiling water. Stir in flour with a wire whisk and slowly beat in milk. Stir constantly until thick, then beat in powdered milk, salt, and pepper. Lower heat and stir in potatoes. Warm and serve.

Twenty-eight

This cheese pudding will surprise you--a bit like a quiche, but simple to cook, delicious and high in protein. You may substitute 3 cups of any cooked whole grain or a mixture of them. If you wish to use white rice, add 3 T wheat germ to the other ingredients.
SERVES 3 OR 4

Crunchy Cheese Pudding

3 cups cooked brown rice
1 cup grated Parmesan
        or Romano cheese
2 eggs
1-1/3 cups milk
1 medium onion, chopped
1/4 cup soy grits
1/2 cup raw peanuts,
        coarsely chopped
1 t dry mustard
1 t salt
1/2 t pepper

Save a bit of cheese to sprinkle on top. Mix all other ingredients in a good sized buttered casserole. Bake 45 minutes in a 325 degree oven. If dinner is late, leave in the cooling oven. It will keep.

Apple Salad with Seeds and Raisins

2 stalks celery
3 apples
1/4 cup sunflower
        kernels
1/3 cup seedless
        raisins
1/2 cup mayonnaise
lettuce

Slice celery. Peel and core apples (or polish and leave unpeeled). Dice apples and mix all ingredients except lettuce in a serving bowl. Make a ring of lettuce around the edge.

56

Twenty-nine

A relative of crunchy cheese pudding. Again--simple and good.
You may substitute your favorite canned bean salad if you wish.
SERVES 4 OR 5

Mushroom and Onion Pudding

3 medium onions, sliced
1/2 lb. mushrooms
4 T butter or margarine
3 cups cooked brown rice
2 eggs
1-1/3 cups milk
1/3 cup powdered milk
1/3 cup unhulled sesame
    seeds
1/2 cup raw peanuts,
    chopped
1 t dry mustard
1 t salt
1/2 t pepper
1/4 t nutmeg

Slice mushrooms. Fry onions in
2 T butter until yellow. Remove
from pan, add remaining butter
and mushrooms. Saute quickly
until brown. Beat milk, eggs,
mustard and powdered milk until
smooth. Mix all ingredients in a
good sized buttered casserole.
Bake one hour in a 325 degree
oven.

Kidney Bean Salad

1 can (16 oz.) kidney
    beans
1 medium onion, chopped
3 stalks celery,
    chopped
1/4 cup vegetable oil
1/4 cup cider vinegar
1 T sugar
1 t salt
1/2 t black pepper

This is best if made the night before but several hours (or even
one) before dinner will do. Drain
the beans and combine in a bowl
with all other ingredients. Cover
and chill.

Thirty

The idea of a bean loaf always makes me think, "Ugh! Vegetarian." But this recipe is really delicious. The only trouble is that it crumbles. We just give up and spoon it out. Double this recipe fills an average loaf pan. Bake the amount given in a smaller pan or casserole. Any creamed vegetable will help to complete the protein and makes a good contrast in textures. Serve with a simple green salad.
SERVES 3 OR 4

Connecticut Bean Loaf

1/4 cup bulgur wheat
1/4 cup water
1 medium onion, minced
1/4 green pepper,
*   minced*
2 T vegetable oil
1 can (16 oz.) kidney
*   beans*
2 eggs
1/2 cup unhulled sesame
*   seeds*
1/4 cup powdered milk
1 t salt
1/2 t pepper
1/8 t garlic powder

Soak bulgur in 1/4 cup water for 1 hour. Brown onion and green pepper in oil. Drain beans, reserving liquid. Beat eggs in a large bowl. Add 1/3 cup bean liquid. Mash beans on a plate with a fork and then mix in the bowl with all other ingredients. Place in greased loaf pan. Pat down with a fork and bake at 350 degrees for 45 minutes.

Thirty-one

Good old potato salad -- with a few changes that raise the protein content. Serve with sliced tomatoes or a tomato aspic.
SERVES 3 OR 4

Potato Salad

3 large potatoes
1 small onion, minced
1 t celery seed
1/2 t salt
1/2 cup French dressing
1/2 cup mayonnaise
1/4 cup yogurt
1/3 cup powdered milk
lettuce

Scrub potatoes, cut out bad spots and peel if you wish. Steam or boil until just tender. Cool and chill. Cut in cubes. Mix all ingredients and serve on a bed of lettuce.

Deviled Eggs

6 hard boiled eggs
2 T French dressing
2 T mayonnaise
2 T powdered milk
1/8 t dry mustard
1/4 t Lea & Perrins
      Worcestershire
      sauce
1 T parsley or chives

Peel eggs and cut in half. Mash yolks & mix with other ingredients. Fill egg whites with the yolk mixture.

Thirty-two

Here is Chow Mein with a touch of West Indian flavor. Use a wok or a large heavy pot. Chinese cooking calls for lots of vegetable slicing, high heat, quick cooking, and stirring.
SERVES 6

Veronica's Chow Mein

1/2 small cabbage
2 cups fresh or canned
        bean sprouts
1 medium onion, sliced
2 carrots
1 green pepper
4 stalks celery
1 clove garlic, minced
2 t powdered ginger
2 t Accent (optional)
1 t pepper
1 T salt
6 T vegetable oil
1 heaping T cornstarch
1 T water

Drain bean sprouts. Slice cabbage very thinly. Core and seed pepper & cut in thin strips. Cut carrots & celery in even thinner strips. Put oil and garlic in pan on high heat. Stir. When hot, add onions and stir. Then carrots, celery and cabbage. Keep stirring. Add salt, pepper, spices and bean sprouts. (Do not use liquid in can.) Stir and cook 4 minutes more. Mix cornstarch and water in a small bowl until smooth. Add and stir until thickened. Serve with a good soy sauce.

Fried Noodles

2 cups egg noodles
1/2 cup vegetable oil
1 cup wheat germ
1 t salt

Put noodles in a large pot with 1 qt. boiling water. Boil 5 minutes. Drain and wash under cold water. Dry on paper towels. When dry, fry until brown in medium hot oil in large frying pan. When noodles are partially browned, stir in wheat germ. When noodles are brown sprinkle with salt, mix & serve.

Thirty-three

Here is an unusual East Indian dinner. It is on the hot side and you may reduce the amount of curry powder if you wish, but do burn the garlic. It sounds crazy, but it makes a big difference. Serve with brown rice and Robert's Cucumbers (Menu twenty-one). SERVES 2 OR 3

Dal of Yellow Split Peas

1/2 cup quick cooking
       yellow split peas
1 quart water
1 small onion, minced
1/8 t garlic powder
2 T vegetable oil
1 t curry powder
1/4 t tumeric
1/4 t cumin powder
1 t salt
1 clove garlic
1 T vegetable oil

Put all ingredients, except the last three listed, in a large saucepan. Boil uncovered for about 1/2 hour or more until peas are all tender and partially mushy. Stir occasionally and add water if needed during cooking. Final consistency should be almost as thick as mashed potatoes. In a heavy pan over high heat cook the garlic clove and oil until the clove is burned. Mix with cooked split peas. Add salt. Let garlic clove stay in until serving time. The Dal may be reheated in a double boiler.

Thirty-four

This is good, easy, and can wait in a cooling oven if dinner is late.
SERVES 2 OR 3

Cheese, Bread and Egg Dish

6 slices whole wheat
    bread
1/2 stick butter or
    margarine
1-1/4 cup grated cheese
2 beaten eggs
1 cup milk
1 t salt
1/2 t paprika
3/4 t dry mustard

Cut bread into small cubes and put in greased casserole. Melt butter and mix with milk and spices. Place in casserole with eggs, bread and 1 cup of cheese. Mix, sprinkle with the rest of the cheese and bake in a 325 degree oven for 30 minutes.

Spinach and Mushroom Salad

Fresh spinach
1 cup fresh mushrooms,
    sliced
1/2 red onion, sliced
1/3 cup unhulled sesame
    seeds
1/4 cup yogurt
1/4 cup French dressing

Remove the tougher stems from enough fresh spinach to make a green salad the size of your appetites. Separate onion rings. Mix all ingredients and toss and serve.

Thirty-five

An unusual and absolutely delicious meal can be made by having plenty of our own bread (Menu Eight) and one of these vegetable combinations.
SERVES 2

Chinese Stir-Fry Vegetables

2 cups sliced asparagus
1-1/2 T vegetable oil
1 t Kikkoman soy sauce
1/2 t salt

Or: 1 cup sliced
*   broccoli*
& 1 cup sliced mush-
*   rooms*

Or: 1 lb. spinach
& 1/2 cup raw peanuts,
*   chopped*

Wash and dry asparagus. (It is very important for vegetables to be dry.) Cut off tough ends. Slice on a sharp diagonal into 1 inch pieces. Set tips aside. Heat wok or heavy pan over high heat. Heat oil & add asparagus. (Reserve tips.) Stir quickly & constantly with 2 spoons for 1-2 minutes. Add tips and cook one minute more. Turn down heat to medium. Stir in soy sauce and salt. Cover & cook 2-3 minutes more.
Broccoli and mushrooms may be done in exactly the same manner. Reserve broccoli flowers and mushroom caps as you did asparagus tips.
Spinach stems should be sliced diagonally in 1/4" slices and cooked 1 minute. Leaves left whole and cooked one minute more without covering. Peanuts should be heated in a pan or oven and added just before serving.

Thirty-six

In general we think it a mistake to make a dish that pretends to be meat, but in the case of sausage, most of the flavor is in the spices not the meat. These are bean patties with sausage flavoring. Use one cup of dry barley, cooked, to help complete the protein in the beans. Barley is usually overlooked except in soups. It is a good change from rice or potato.
SERVES 2 OR 3

Sausage Patties without Meat

```
1 can (16 oz.) white
     limas ( or other
     white beans)
1/4 cup soy grits
1/4 cup rolled oats
1 t salt
1/2 t pepper
1 t sage
1/8 t garlic powder
1/4 t ginger
3 T vegetable oil
```

Drain beans, reserving liquid. Mash beans on a plate with a fork. Mix beans and all other ingredients in a large bowl. Add some liquid if the mixture is too dry. Shape into patties and fry in oil--or in bacon fat, if you have some that would otherwise go to waste.

Creamed Carrots with Celery Seeds

```
6 large carrots
2 T butter
1 T flour
3/4 cup milk
2/3 cup powdered milk
1/4 t salt
1/4 t pepper
1/2 t celery seeds
```

Cut carrots in pieces. Steam or boil until just tender. Melt butter in a saucepan over medium heat. Stir in flour with a wire whisk and keep stirring until thickened. Add milk, milk powder, and spices and stir until smooth. Add carrots. Add extra milk if too thick. Reheat if needed and serve.

Thirty-seven

This is an unusual meal and a good one for serving vegetarian food to guests. You may serve with Italian bread, if you wish, but the noodles are filling.
SERVES 3 OR 4

Joel's Noodles

1 stick butter or
        margarine
2/3 cup of milk
4 T powdered milk
1/2 lb. medium noodles
2 t salt
1 cup grated Parmesan
        cheese
1/4 cup wheat germ
2/3 cup raw peanuts,
        chopped
1/2 t medium grind
        black pepper

Melt butter in a small pan and add milk and powdered milk. Put noodles and salt in 3 quarts boiling water. Cook 6-7 minutes. Drain well and return to pan over very low heat. Add butter mixture and cheese, a little at a time, tossing gently after each addition. Stir in wheat germ, peanuts, and pepper and serve immediately. (If you have to reheat, add milk to moisten.)

Winter or Summer Spinach Salad

Fresh spinach
1/3 cup unhulled sesame
        seeds
1 cup sliced mushrooms
        (or 2 sliced
        tomatoes)
1 red onion, sliced
Italian dressing

Wash, dry, and trim spinach. Add other ingredients, according to season, toss and serve.

Thirty-eight

Stuff the peppers early on a lazy summer day. You can even get the wet and dry muffin ingredients all ready to combine and bake them just before dinner. Serve with sliced tomatoes.
SERVES 3 OR 4

Selden's Stuffed Green Pepper Salad

```
1/2 cup chopped
      cucumber
2 carrots, finely
      chopped
1/4 cup sunflower
      kernels
1/4 cup chopped chives
1/2 t thyme
1 envelope plain
      gelatin
2 T water
1/4 cup boiling water
1/2 cup mayonnaise
2 cups creamed cottage
      cheese
4 or 5 green peppers,
      cored and seeded
lettuce
French dressing
```

Prepare vegetables. Soak gelatin in 2 T water in large bowl. When all moist, dissolve by adding 1/4 cup boiling water and stirring well. Add mayonnaise, stirring quickly as it may begin to gel. Stir in other ingredients, also quickly. Fill green peppers, place upright in a dish and chill for 2 hours. Cut salad rings, 1/2 to 3/4 of an inch wide. Serve with French dressing on a bed of lettuce.

Jane's Peanut Muffins

```
1-1/2 cups whole wheat
      flour
1/2 cup rolled oats
1/2 cup raw peanuts,
      chopped
3 t baking powder
1/2 t salt
2 eggs
1/4 cup vegetable oil
1/4 cup brown sugar
1 cup milk
```

Combine dry ingredients. Combine wet ingredients and beat until brown sugar is fairly well blended in. Mix everything together quickly. Ignore lumps. Fill greased muffin tins about 1/3 full. Bake in preheated 400 degree oven for about 20 minutes.

66

Thirty-nine

Polenta is a common dish among the Italian poor--but not usually in as elaborate a version as ours. Mushrooms are high in protein on their own, and the combination makes for a robust dish. We suggest serving with broccoli or Brussels sprouts. Leftovers are good reheated with zucchini or peas.
SERVES 5 OR 6

Polenta with Cheese and Mushrooms

```
1 lb. mushrooms, sliced
4 T vegetable oil
2 quarts water
1 T salt
2 cups cornmeal
1/4 cup powdered milk
1-1/4 cups grated
        Parmesan cheese
1/2 cup milk
1/2 cup unhulled
        sesame seeds
```

Cook and stir mushrooms in oil over high heat for 4 minutes. Set aside. Bring water and salt to a boil in a large pan. Lower to medium heat and gradually add cornmeal while stirring constantly with a wooden spoon. Cook and stir for 10 minutes, then add powdered milk and keep stirring for 10 more minutes. Mixture should be smooth. Remove from heat & stir in milk, seeds, and mushrooms. Put in a shallow greased casserole, sprinkle cheese on top, and bake in a 350 degree oven for 40 minutes.

Forty

Tabouli is a Mid-Eastern salad. If you have a soup tureen (a large bowl or casserole will do as well) and a ladle, you can bring the soup to the table, along with the tabouli arranged on a decorative salad plate, and let people help themselves.
SERVES 4 OR 5

Tabouli

1 cup raw bulgur
1 cup minced fresh
    parsley
1/2 cup chopped
    mint (optional)
1 medium onion, minced
grated rind 1 lemon
2 T lemon juice
1/4 cup olive oil
1/2 t salt
1/4 t cracked black
    pepper
4 ripe tomatoes
1 cup cottage cheese
French dressing

Pour about 3 cups of boiling water over the bulgur and let stand 2 hours. Drain very well. Then mix all ingredients, except tomatoes and cottage cheese, in a bowl. Chill. Chop two of the tomatoes in small pieces and mix in. Arrange on a plate with bulgur in the center and alternate mounds of cottage cheese and tomato wedges around the edge. Serve with French dressing for the extra tomatoes and cottage cheese.

Hearty Curry Soup

2 carrots
1 medium onion
3 T butter or margarine
2 t curry powder
1 box frozen peas
1 can (16 oz.) white
    beans (limas,
    cannelini, etc.)
1 can condensed cream
    of celery soup
1 can milk
1 t salt
2 T sherry (optional)

Chop the carrots and onion finely. Cook in butter until soft. Add curry powder and cook a minute longer. Cook peas and drain. Blend beans (include liquid) and milk in blender one minute. (Or put through food mill) Mix all ingredients except peas in a large saucepan and heat. Add peas a minute before serving.

68

Forty-one

Do use green split peas instead of yellow! They look better with cornbread. You may substitute a mix with milk. If it contains none, sprinkle 1/4 cup sesame seeds on the top of the mix before baking. A Waldorf Salad, or other fruit salad, makes a good accompaniment.
SERVES 3 OR 4

Split Pea Soup with Vegetables

1 cup quick cooking
    split peas
4 cups water
1 bay leaf
1 carrot, chopped
2 stalks celery,
    chopped
1 medium onion
1/2 t salt
pepper to taste
1 t dill or caraway
    seeds

Pick over peas and wash. Combine peas, water and bay leaf in a large pot. Bring to a boil, lower heat, and simmer until almost tender (about 20 minutes). Remove from heat. Force about 1/2 of the soup through a strainer or food mill, or blend in a blender. Return this to the soup pot, add seasonings, seeds, & chopped vegetables. Simmer 15-20 minutes more until vegetables are soft but not mushy.

Cornbread with Sesame Seeds

1/2 cup flour
3 t baking powder
1 t salt
1 cup yellow corn meal
1/4 cup wheat germ
1/4 cup powdered milk
3/4 cup milk
1/4 cup honey
2 eggs, slightly beaten
2 T vegetable oil
1/3 cup unhulled sesame
    seeds

Mix together flour, baking powder, salt, cornmeal, wheat germ & powdered milk. Add to the dry ingredients the milk, honey, slightly beaten eggs and vegetable oil. Beat well with a wooden spoon for about 1 minute. Pour into a greased 8" x 8" pan, sprinkle sesame seeds on top and bake in a preheated oven at 425 degrees for 20-25 minutes.

69

Forty-two

Even though these lentil cakes have curry in them they won't taste like it, but as the title implies, they will taste mildly spiced. If you use a hot curry powder the taste will change. These are very hearty foods and a simple green salad will complete the meal. SERVES 2

Mildly Spiced Lentil Cakes

1/2 cup uncooked
        lentils
2 cups water
1 medium onion, chopped
1 T butter or margarine
2 t salt
2 t mild curry powder
1/4 cup powdered milk
1/4 cup wheat germ
1/2 cup whole wheat
        flour
2 T vegetable oil

Bring lentils to a boil, lower heat & simmer until lentils are tender but not mushy (40-60 minutes). If you run out of water before lentils are tender, add a bit and stir. Fry onion in butter until soft. Drain beans, reserving liquid. Put beans in a bowl and mash slightly with fork. Add all other ingredients but oil. Mix with enough bean liquid to make mixture like soft mashed potatoes. Brown large spoonfuls of bean mixture on both sides in oil over medium heat.

Muriel's Creamed Onions and Peanuts

1 can (16 oz.) onions
2 T butter or margarine
2 T flour
1 cup milk
1/2 cup raw peanuts,
        chopped
1/2 t salt
1 t chopped parsley

Drain onions. Melt butter in top of a double boiler. Add flour & stir with wire whisk until smooth. Gradually add milk, stirring constantly until mixture thickens. Add onions, salt, parsley, and peanuts and stir until blended. Heat and serve.

Forty-three

Here are two recipes apt to be popular with young children as well as adults.
SERVES 3 OR 4

Oats, Tomatoes and Cheese

2 cups rolled oats
1 cup grated cheese
1 can (16 oz.) tomatoes
1 egg
1 cup milk
1 t salt
1/2 t pepper
1 t marjoram

Save some cheese for the top. Mix all other ingredients in a greased casserole. Sprinkle with cheese and bake for 1 hour at 325 degrees.

Green Bean Casserole

2 packages frozen green
    beans
3 T butter or margarine
2 T flour
1 cup sour cream
1 t salt
1 t sugar
1/3 cup wheat germ
3 slices Swiss cheese

Boil or steam green beans. Drain & place in greased casserole. Melt butter & stir in flour. Add sour cream slowly, beating with a wire whisk until thick and smooth. Stir in salt & sugar. Pour this mixture over the green beans. Sprinkle with wheat germ & top with cheese. Bake covered in a 325 degree oven for 20 minutes. Uncover and bake 15 minutes longer.

Forty-four

This is a simple meal that will seem familiar and yet provides a good deal of protein. The wheat germ puts back in nutrition what was polished out of the flour, and the soy grits, together with the cheese, do a good job of helping to complete the protein. Serve with a green salad and Italian bread, butter or margarine.
SERVES 6

Spaghetti Marinara

4 medium onions,
     chopped
1 green pepper, chopped
4 T vegetable oil
6 cups marinara sauce
     (3 16 oz. jars)
1/3 cup wheat germ
1/2 cup soy grits
2/3 cup Parmesan cheese
2 T chopped parsley
1 lb. extra thin or
     thin spaghetti
extra grated Parmesan
     cheese

Cook onions and green pepper in oil until soft. Add sauce, wheat germ, soy grits, cheese and parsley. Simmer several minutes, stirring often. Cook spaghetti about 7 minutes, but do not overcook. It should be on the firm side. Drain well. Spoon sauce over spaghetti. Be generous. Top each portion with Parmesan cheese.

Forty-five

You can get excellent canned Boston baked beans and this saves hours of time and fuel. There is usually a small bit of salt pork in the beans, but it seems scrupulous to be concerned about it. We have, therefore, concentrated on recipes to go with the beans.
SERVES 4 OR 5

Boston Brown Bread

1 cup whole wheat flour
1 cup cornmeal
3/4 cup powdered milk
1 t salt
4 t baking powder
1-1/2 cups raisins
2 cups milk
1 cup molasses

This makes 3 small loaves. Mix dry ingredients, stir in raisins and then add milk and molasses and stir well. Pour into 3 well-greased 16 oz. tin cans. Fill 2/3 full. Cover cans with brown paper and tie with string. Place on a rack in a large pot. Fill pot with boiling water to come half way up cans. Cover pot & steam bread for 2 hours. Let cool in cans before removing.

Cole Slaw

4 cups shredded cabbage
1 small onion, finely
        chopped
1 t celery seeds
1/2 cup yogurt
1/2 cup mayonnaise
1/4 cup French dressing

Mix well and serve.

Forty-six

Surely cheese souffle is one of the most delicate and yet satisfying
of dishes. The macaroni salad helps to complete the protein.
SERVES 4

Cheese Souffle

```
1-1/2 cups milk
3 T margarine
3 T flour
1-1/2 cups sharp cheese
       grated
1-1/2 t salt
1/2 t paprika
1/2 cup powdered milk
4 eggs, separated
```

Heat milk. Melt butter & beat
in flour with wire whisk. Add
milk slowly while stirring. Stir
until it thickens. Add cheese,
powdered milk, salt & paprika.
Stir until cheese is melted. Remove from heat and cool slightly. Beat egg yolks until lemon-
colored & stir quickly into sauce.
Beat egg whites until stiff and
fold in gently. Pour into a
1-1/2 qt., straight sided, un-
greased baking dish & bake in
preheated 300 degree oven for
45 or 50 minutes. Serve
immediately.

Macaroni Salad

```
1 cup macaroni
1 cup French dressing
1/2 cup wheat germ
1/4 cup soy grits
1/3 cup fresh parsley
1 medium onion, minced
1/2 cup raw peanuts
2 tomatoes, chopped
2 stalks celery, chopped
1/4 cup unhulled sesame
       seeds
```

Boil macaroni until just tender.
Drain, and while still hot, mix
with salad dressing. Cool.
Chop parsley, peanuts & other
vegetables. Mix with other ingredients and chill.

Forty-seven

Here is a recipe for a classic Southern spoon bread, very light in texture. The okra dish is more unusual. If you like okra, try it. If not, you may substitute any one of our bean recipes. You may wish to serve a green salad also.
SERVES 3 OR 4

Spoon Bread

2 cups milk
1 cup cornmeal
1 t salt
1 t sugar
2 T butter
2 beaten egg yolks
2 t baking powder
2 stiffly beaten
*   egg whites*

Bring milk to a simmer, stir in cornmeal quickly. Remove from heat and mix in butter, salt, and sugar. Let cool 1/2 hour. Beat in egg yolks and baking powder and then carefully fold in egg whites. Put in a greased casserole and bake in preheated 350 degree oven for 45 minutes or until brown on top. Serve immediately.

Tomatoes and Okra

1 box frozen okra
1 medium onion, chopped
2 T butter or margarine
1 can (16 oz.) tomatoes
1/2 cup raw peanuts,
*   chopped*
1 t salt
1/2 t pepper
1/8 t garlic powder
2 T soy grits

Defrost okra. Cook onion in butter until soft & then combine all ingredients in a large saucepan. Bring to a boil & simmer 10 minutes.

Forty-eight

The soup is simple, the popovers delicious. A salad of coleslaw with chopped apples goes well with this meal. Choose red apples, polish, and leave the skins on.
SERVES 3

Quick Bean Soup

2 carrots, minced
2 T butter or margarine
1 can (16 oz.) kidney
    beans
1 can condensed mush-
    room soup
2 T parsley
1 t marjoram
1 t celery seed
1 t salt
1 cup milk
1/3 cup powdered milk

The carrots should be finely minced. Cook them in butter until almost tender. Put all ingredients, including bean liquid, in a large saucepan. Mix, heat, and serve.

Whole Wheat Popovers

3 eggs
1 cup milk
1 cup whole wheat flour
1/2 t salt

Beat eggs 3 minutes. Stir in milk. Add flour & salt and beat for 1/2 minute. Scrape sides of bowl & beat 2 minutes longer. (A blender takes less time.) Grease six 6-oz. Pyrex custard cups and divide batter between them. Space evenly on cookie sheet in preheated 400 degree oven. Bake 30-40 minutes until richly brown. If baked in preheated popover pan, allow only 25-30 minutes.)

Forty-nine

This is a reasonably hot curry. Leave out the chili powder if you like. Be sure to serve with brown rice to help complete the protein in the curry.
SERVES 2 OR 3

Curried Vegetables

1 can (16 oz.) white
     limas (or other
     beans)
1 medium onion, chopped
1/2 cup chopped celery
1 package of frozen
     vegetables
     (mixed or green
     or yellow)
1/4 cup unhulled sesame
     seeds
4 T butter or margarine
1 T curry powder
1 t chili powder
1/8 t garlic powder

Drain beans and put liquid into a saucepan. Cook onion and celery in butter until onion is almost tender. Add curry, chili and garlic and cook a few seconds longer. Combine with bean liquid and add frozen vegetables and sesame seeds. Cook until tender and add beans. Cook 3 minutes longer.

Carrot Salad

5 large carrots
1/2 green pepper
1/4 cup mayonnaise
1/4 cup yogurt

Grate the carrots. Cut the green pepper in slivers and mix with the mayonnaise and yogurt.

Fifty

This is a good meal for a cold winter's night. Serve with a green salad or any green vegetable.
SERVES 3 OR 4

Crunchy Bean Patties

1/4 green pepper,
    chopped
1 medium onion, chopped
1 T butter or margarine
1 can (16 oz.) kidney
    beans
1/2 cup whole wheat
    flour
1 egg
1 t salt
1/2 cup unhulled sesame
    seeds
4 T vegetable oil

Fry pepper and onion lightly in butter. Drain beans (reserving liquid), put in a bowl, mash slightly with a potato masher or fork. Stir in flour and 1/3 cup bean liquid. Beat egg slightly and add to bean mixture with salt sesame seeds, onion and green pepper. Mix well. Heat oil in frying pan. Drop bean mixture by large spoonfuls into pan and fry until brown on both sides.

Scalloped Potatoes

3 large potatoes
1-1/4 cups milk
2 T butter or margarine
2 T flour
1-1/4 cups grated
    cheese
1 t salt
1/2 t paprika
1/3 cup powdered milk

Scrub potatoes well and cut out any bad spots. Peel if desired & slice very thin. Melt butter in large saucepan. Stir in flour with a wire whisk. Add milk slowly and stir until thick and smooth. Add paprika, salt, cheese, powdered milk and potatoes. Mix well and pour into a greased casserole. Bake at 325 degrees for two hours or until potatoes are tender.

Fifty-one

Timbales are rather neglected these days. They are a bit of trouble to turn out of the mold but well worth it. Serve these with rice or bulgur, to help complete the protein, and a tomato salad. SERVES 3 OR 4

Broccoli Timbales

2 cups cooked broccoli
4 eggs
2 cups milk
1/4 cup herb stuffing
        mix
1/2 t salt
1/4 t paprika
1/4 t lemon juice

Chop cooked broccoli very fine. Beat eggs and stir in other ingredients. Add broccoli and spoon into greased timbale molds, custard cups, or ring mold. Bake in preheated oven in shallow pan of hot water (also pre-heated) at 325 degrees for about 20 minutes for small molds and 30 for a large mold or until firm. Unmold and serve with cheese sauce.

Cheese Sauce

2 T butter or margarine
2 T flour
1-1/2 cups milk
1-1/2 cups grated sharp
        cheese
1/2 t salt
1/4 t paprika
1/2 t dry mustard

Melt butter in top of a double boiler. Stir in flour with a wire whisk. Heat milk in a saucepan and slowly add to margarine and flour, stirring until thick. Add cheese and flavorings and cook until cheese is melted, stirring occasionally.

Fifty-two

This is a good summer menu when the zucchinis are plentiful and tomatoes fresh. Serve these dishes with a plate of sliced ripe tomatoes.
SERVES 4

Stuffed Zucchini

4 zucchini (5-6")
1 medium onion
2 T butter or margarine
1 tomato, peeled and
      chopped
2 T parsley
1 t oregano
1/2 t salt
1/4 t pepper
1/4 cup sunflower
      kernels
1/3 cup herb stuffing
      crumbs
1/3 cup Parmesan cheese
butter

Drop zucchini into boiling water. Remove after 3 minutes. Drain, cool & halve lengthwise. Scoop out pulp, leaving the shells 1/4" thick. Saute onion & chopped pulp in butter. When tender add next 7 ingredients. Then spoon filling into shells. Top with Parmesan cheese. Dot tops with butter. Cover and bake in 375 degree oven about 15 minutes, until fork tender. Uncover and place under broiler to crisp cheese.

Middle Eastern Salad

1 cup uncooked lentils
3 whole cloves
2 cups boiling water
grated rind 1 orange
1 medium onion, chopped
1 clove garlic, minced
2 T vegetable oil
1 t salt
1/4 t black pepper
1/4 cup olive oil
juice of 1 lemon (4 T)

Simmer lentils, cloves & orange rind in water in a covered pan for 30 minutes or until tender. (Add water if needed to prevent sticking. Drain any water remaining after cooking.) Fry onion and garlic in oil until golden. Mix with lentils and chill. Mix in last ingredients & serve on a bed of greens.

Breakfast, Lunch & Leftovers

More and more in recent years, doctors and nutritionists have been telling us that breakfast is the most important meal of the day. In particular they stress the need for protein at breakfast. When little protein is consumed at the start of the day, fatigue follows later in the day. The less protein, the earlier the fatigue. Without discussing the pros and cons of additional non-protein breakfast foods such as coffee and orange juice, we would like to make some suggestions about breakfast proteins.

Many instant (and non-instant) hot cereals are available on the market. We suggest that you pick your favorite cereal and increase its usable protein value by combining it in one of the following ways, or by using our chart on Page 21 and following your fancy. In either case, take a box of cereal, measure it by cups, add the given amounts of the suggested ingredients and put in a large jar ready for use. When cooking, you may need more water than usual.

To 3 cups whole grain cereal add 1-1/3 cups powdered milk.

To 3 cups non whole grain cereal add 1-1/3 cups powdered milk and 1/2 cup wheat germ.

To 3 cups whole grain cereal add 1/4 cup soy grits, 1/2 cup chopped peanuts, 1/2 cup powdered milk and 1/3 cup raisins.

(Remember to add extra water if needed while cooking.)

If all you can get your family to eat is orange juice and toast, try our Crunchy Whole Wheat Bread on Menu Eight--it has the milk in it. Or give them any whole wheat bread and a glass of milk. Even a breakfast with eggs (or Eggbeaters) will have more usable protein if the toast that goes with the eggs is whole grain and made with a high proportion of milk.

Many of our menus can also be used for lunch when you wish to serve a fairly elaborate meal (or for supper if dinner is in the middle of the day). If you wish a lighter meal, check the protein balances in individual dishes within the menu against our chart. If they are reasonably balanced without the other foods suggested in the menu, they could be served alone or with a lighter accompaniment. Egg dishes, of course, are excellent protein by themselves.

But most lunches these days are apt to be casual affairs of soup and/or sandwich. Two of the most common sandwiches served in America are amazingly well supplied with the essential eight (considering how often our breakfasts are not). These two are a cheese sandwich and a peanut butter sandwich. All you really need to do is to use some sort of whole grain bread. Variations on cheese or peanut butter sandwiches abound so we will not discuss them here, nor the need for some accompanying fruit or vegetable. Some delicious sandwiches can be made from leftover bean dishes. Mash the beans and moisten with catsup or mayonnaise, or whatever seems sensible and use as a sandwich spread.

If packing lunchboxes, one of the easiest and most appealing things to do, is to make any whole grain sandwich you wish and then include a bag of peanuts. If milk, or a milk based soup, is in the lunch box, try a bag of sunflower kernels.

Any of our soups may be reheated for lunch, and you can stretch them with whatever leftover vegetables you have on hand, or thin them with milk or tomato juice. Just take a glance at our chart, and see if you should have some toast with the soup, or throw in some leftover cooked grain.

If you are on a diet, one of the simplest and best meals is to take leftover salad and mix it with cottage cheese. If it doesn't have beans, seeds, grains or peanuts in it already, sprinkle on a few, season a bit and mix. It sounds terrible, but it is usually good, quick and sustaining, without adding too many calories. And yogurt — when you help to complete the protein with peanuts or whole grain bread — makes for an even simpler lunch.

If you always lunch out and are faced with leftover vegetarian dishes and don't know what to do with them, we have several suggestions. Many will freeze well, most particularly the moister dishes such as soups and vegetable casseroles. Many will mix well with other leftovers and make a new casserole for another meal. This is particularly true of vegetable and grain combinations.

Our last suggestion is a bit heretical, but since this book is meant to save protein food, rather than merely to eliminate meat from our diets, we suggest that you can combine some leftovers with small amounts of meat into quite new dishes. After all, if the same vegetable protein principles are applied and meat is added, it just means that you have a good protein meal instead of a bit of meat mixed with this or that (which may or may not result in sufficient protein). For instance, suppose you had some leftover Joel's Noodles (Menu Thirty-seven) you could take them from the freezer, defrost and remoisten with a bit of milk. Then add some scraps of leftover ham, warm in the double boiler, make a fresh salad, and there you are. Meat stocks should certainly not be forgotten either. Although it's getting harder to get bones these days, there is always the chicken carcass. Boil it in water for an hour and strain. Reserve the bits of meat and add leftover — well, I wouldn't add leftover Raisin Bran Muffins — but an amazing number of our recipes could be mixed with a good chicken stock and become a hearty soup for another meal.

Useful Cookbooks

DIET FOR A SMALL PLANET by Frances Moore Lappe, Ballantine Books, N.Y., 1971, 1975 (revised) in paper. $1.95.

We believe this book will eventually have at least as much impact on the world as Rachel Carson's SILENT SPRING and probably more. Although it has a good many recipes, it is not primarily a cookbook but a serious, yet readable, study of the world's food resources, particularly with regard to protein. As Ms. Lappe points out, she "was amazed to learn that much of the critical study of plant protein is just now beginning to be done." (1971) If you want to really understand how to get the most out of vegetable protein, this is the book to read.

RECIPES FOR A SMALL PLANET by Ellen Buchman Ewald, Ballantine Books, N.Y., 1973. $1.50 in paper.

Written by Frances Lappe's friend, this is a cookbook based on the principles explained in the earlier book. There are good charts and other useful sections. Ingredients are sometimes unfamiliar and preparation time sometimes long. Otherwise excellent.

GREAT MEATLESS MEALS by Frances Moore Lappe & Ellen Buchman Ewald, Ballantine, N.Y., 1974. $1.50 in paper.

The recipes in the above two books arranged in menu form.

COOKING WHAT COMES NATURALLY by Nikki Goldbeck, Cornerstone Library, N.Y., 1973. $1.95 in paper.

Although this book pays little attention to protein, it is an otherwise excellent vegetarian cookbook. As its title implies, the emphasis is on natural foods.

GOOD FOOD WITHOUT MEAT by Ann Seranne, Wm. Morrow & Co., Inc., N.Y., 1973. $8.95 in hardcover.

Gourmet vegetarian cooking. Some superb dishes but not enough attention to protein.

VEGETABLE PROTEIN and VEGETARIAN COOKBOOK by Jeanne Larson & Ruth McLin, Arco, 1974. $6.95 in hardcover.

Like ours it has 52 menus and uses beans, grains, milk, and eggs. Unlike ours it does not pay much attention to the essential amino acids.

TASSAJARA COOKING by Edward Espe Brown, Shambhala, Berkley, 1973. $3.95 in paper.
From the Zen Center. A beautiful book that will increase your love of vegetables. Little about protein.

THE TASSAJARA BREAD BOOK by Edward Espe Brown, Shambhala, Berkley, 1970. $3.50 in paper.
Bread cooked with whole grain flours and milk powder is rich in protein. This superb bread book tells you how.

THE NEW YORK TIMES NATURAL FOODS COOKBOOK by Jean Hewitt, Avon, N.Y., 1971. $1.95 in paper.
Although the emphasis — again — is on natural foods, there are many well balanced vegetable protein dishes. Not a totally vegetarian book.

THE BENEVOLENT BEAN by Margaret and Ancel Keys, Noonday Press, N.Y., 1972. $2.45 in paper.
The Keys' main interest was low cholesterol, but in the process they produced some excellent bean recipes. First published in 1967 they did not have access to the latest protein research, so consult our book or Lappe or Moore when adapting recipes.

LET'S COOK IT RIGHT by Adelle Davis, Harcourt, New Am. Library, N.Y., 1962. $1.75 in paper.
Those who know of Adelle Davis only as a writer on vitamins and health should meet her as a cook. No one explains more clearly why and how things cook and what happens to the nutrients.

THE JOY OF COOKING by Irma S. Rombauer, New Am. Library, N.Y. 1 vol. ed. $3.95 in paper.
This is the book that really introduced America to "the casserole". The hardcover editions brought out during the

Second World War meat shortage have useful suggestions.

FANNIE FARMER BOSTON COOKING SCHOOL COOKBOOK
by Wilma L. Perkins, Bantam, N.Y., 1970. $1.50 in paper.
This old classic--just because it is old--has some valuable recipes from simpler times. The older hardcover
editions are the most useful.

AMINO-ACID CONTENT OF FOODS AND BIOLOGICAL DATA
ON PROTEINS, Food and Agriculture Organization of the
United Nations, UNIPUB, 650 First Ave., P.O. Box 453,
N.Y. 10016, 1970. $15.00 in paper.
If you are a nutritionist or biologist and want a source book
on vegetable protein, here is an exhaustive series of tables.
Extremely difficult for the layman to follow.

Growing Your Own

A number of vegetable protein foods are easily grown by the home gardener. We would like to mention a few and, rather than go into gardening or preserving methods here, we have appended a bibliography of useful books.

SUNFLOWERS need a sunny place but thrive in almost any soil. Some varieties are short but most are 5-6' tall. We didn't mention PUMPKIN SEEDS in the recipes, but they can be used in place of sunflower seeds. There is a variety with hulless seeds specially developed for the seed. Suitably they are called "Lady Godiva."

PEANUTS take a good deal of space and require a long growing season but will grow as far North as New York state. They prefer a loose soil.

BEANS and PEAS can be grown in many varieties. The only reason that you can't rely on fresh beans and peas for protein is comparative water content. (Imagine the bulk of a box of split peas if they were the size of fresh peas.) But any of them can be dried if you wish to take the trouble. Pole beans are fun and take little room. Soy beans need a long growing season but Early Green Bush and Giant Green will do well in New England as well as the South. Fava, or Broad beans, like cool weather and are a good variety for drying.

MUSHROOMS can be grown winter or summer. In summer they can be grown in a corner of your lawn! (See "The Basic Book of Organic Gardening") In winter watch for ads of boxes prepared for growing mushrooms in your cellar.

SOYBEAN SPROUTS can also be grown in the house (See "Tassajara Cooking" on our cookbook list), but their nutritional content is quite different than soybeans. They go down in protein value, but are rich in vitamins. And delicious.

If you don't know much of anything about gardening or just want a clear and ready reference try: VEGETABLE GARDENING, Sunset Books, Menlo Park, Cal., $1.95 in paper. There are less helpful pictures in SMALL FRUIT AND VEGETABLE GARDENS by Jaqueline Heriteau, Popular Library, $1.50 in paper, but there is more information.

If you know a little about gardening but not as much as you'd like about organic gardening, THE BASIC BOOK OF ORGANIC GARDENING, ed. by Robert Rodale, Ballantine, $1.25 in paper, is the most thorough and reliable on the market. The Rodales were the pioneers in the field. 300 OF THE MOST ASKED QUESTIONS ABOUT ORGANIC GARDENING, Bantam, $1.25 in paper, is just what it sounds like. The questions came to, and were answered by, the editors of ORGANIC GARDENING MAGAZINE, which is also a Rodale publication. (Rodale Press, 33 East Minor St., Emmaus, Pa., 18049)

Two books that are delightful and informative reading on special subjects are: HOW TO HAVE A GREEN THUMB WITHOUT AN ACHING BACK: A new method of mulch gardening, by Ruth Stout, Cornerstone, $1.95 in paper. Mrs. Stout is an avid gardener, who, when getting on in years, wished to save time and energy. PEACOCK MANURE AND MARIGOLDS: A no-poison guide to a beautiful garden, by Janet Gillespie, Ballantine, $1.25 in paper, is equally delightful to read. As the sub-title implies, it is about how to scare away the bugs without the use of injurious poisons.

If you grow some of your own vegetable protein, you may also be interested in preserving it. PUTTING FOOD BY by Hertzberg, Vaughn & Greene, Stephen Greene Press, Brattleboro, 1973, $3.95 in paper is clear, scientific and covers all the major methods of preserving foods. PRESERVING THE FRUITS OF THE EARTH by Schuler & Schuler, Dial Press, 1973, $6.95 in paper, covers many more foods. Not only basic ones, but bluefish, hickory nuts, buffalo berries and foods we've never heard of. Fun reading as well as useful.

Sources of Unusual Ingredients

The only ingredients listed in our recipes that are not available in most markets are usually in stock in any health food
store. If there is none in your neighborhood, or you wish to
buy in bulk, here are some addresses of mail order houses.
Besides raw peanuts, sunflower kernels, unhulled sesame
seeds, bulgur, and soy grits, they carry other foods such as
whole grain flours and organically grown foods.

WALNUT ACRES, Penns Creek, Pa., 17862 is an old and
reliable firm with an excellent reputation.

EL MOLINO MILLS, 345 N. Baldwin Park Blvd., City of
Industry, California, 91746, has a good catalog.

EREWHON TRADING COMPANY, INC., 342 Newbury St.,
Boston, Mass., 02115 OR 8003 Beverly Blvd., Los Angeles,
Calif., 90048. Newer but reliable. Sends by UPS or other
means, not by mail. Good prices for bulk buying.

Index

Related Seabury Titles
Available in Paperback

GARDENING WITH CONSCIENCE: The Organic-Intensive
Method by Marny Smith. Foreword by Joan Gussow; Illustrated
by Frances Boynton. A year-'round guide to gardening using
step-by-step methods adaptable to all parts of the country; an
enrichment for family life.

LET THE EARTH BLESS THE LORD by C. A. Cesaretti and
Stephen Commins, Editors. A challenging resource book for
Chritian adult discussion groups wishing to study the problem of
land use today.

LIVING SIMPLY: An Examination of Christian Lifestyles
by David Crean and Eric and Helen Ebbeson, Editors. Authors
from several denominations write for ordinary Christians who
wish to consider lifestyle issues, community life, and change.